D0574716

21st Century
Basic Skills
Library

PATTERNS IN THE CITY

by Rebecca Felix

Cherry Lake Publishing • Ann Arbor, Michigan

2

Published in the United States of America
by Cherry Lake Publishing
Ann Arbor, Michigan
www.cherrylakepublishing.com

Consultants: Janice A. Bradley, PhD; Marla Conn, ReadAbility, Inc.

Editorial direction and book production: Red Line Editorial

Photo Credits: iStockphoto, cover, 1; Paul Prescott/Shutterstock Images, 4; iStock/Thinkstock, 6, 12; James Hardy/Thinkstock, 8; Shutterstock Images, 10; Nicholas Belton/iStock/Thinkstock, 14; Jowita Stachowiak/iStock/Thinkstock, 16; Botond Horvath/Shutterstock Images, 18; Jolanta Vaitkeviciene/iStock/Thinkstock, 20

Library of Congress Cataloging-in-Publication Data
Felix, Rebecca, 1984-
  Patterns in the city / by Rebecca Felix.
     pages cm. -- (Patterns all around)
  Includes index.
  ISBN 978-1-63188-922-6 (hardcover : alk. paper) -- ISBN 978-1-63188-938-7 (pbk. : alk. paper) -- ISBN 978-1-63188-954-7 (pdf) -- ISBN 978-1-63188-970-7 (hosted ebook)
 1. Pattern perception--Juvenile literature. 2. Shapes--Juvenile literature. 3. Cities and towns--Juvenile literature. I. Title.

 BF294.F455 2015
 152.14'23--dc23

                          2014030121

Cherry Lake Publishing would like to acknowledge the work of The Partnership for 21st Century Skills. Please visit *www.p21.org* for more information.

Printed in the United States of America
Corporate Graphics
December 2014

TABLE OF CONTENTS

4

Patterns

Patterns are all around the city! Patterns are things that **repeat**. These windows repeat.

How many times does this pattern's core repeat?

Pattern **cores** repeat twice or more. They repeat in **order**. This city sign's core is yellow, black.

What Do You See?

Do you see the pattern on Eli's toy hoop?

City Parks

City parks have space to play. Eli runs on a pattern.

Call white A. Call blue B. The core is AB.

Letters help show cores. Jax skateboards on an ABC pattern at a city park.

Sage colors the sidewalk. It is a city **walkway**.

The colors do not repeat in order. They do *not* make a pattern.

What's Next?

Some triangles on this **skyscraper** point up. Call them A. Others point down. Call them B.

The core is AB. **Predict** what follows AB.

This city roadwork shows many patterns. One begins rectangle, cone. What's next?

This city playground fence shows an ABCD pattern. Green follows red. What follows yellow?

What Do You See?

How many patterns do you see?

City patterns are also found on people!

Find Out More

BOOK

Steggall, Susan. *Red Car, Red Bus.* London: Frances Lincoln-First Trade, 2015.

WEB SITE

ABCYa.com—Moon Rock Patterns
www.abcya.com/patterns.htm
Play a fun game predicting what comes next in color patterns.

Glossary

cores (KORZ) the smallest repeating parts of patterns

order (OR-dur) set in a repeating way

predict (pree-DIKT) to say what will come next or in the future

repeat (ri-PEET) to appear or happen again and again

skyscraper (SKYE-skray-pur) a very tall building

walkway (WAWK-way) a path for walking

Home and School Connection

Use this list of words from the book to help your child become a better reader. Word games and writing activities can help beginning readers reinforce literacy skills.

begins	green	playground	skateboards
black	hoop	point	skyscraper
blue	letters	predict	space
call	make	rectangle	things
city	next	red	times
colors	one	repeat	triangles
cone	order	roadwork	twice
core	parks	runs	walkway
fence	patterns	show	white
follows	people	sidewalk	windows
found	play	sign	yellow

What Do You See?

What Do You See? is a feature paired with select photos in this book. It encourages young readers to interact with visual images in order to build the ability to integrate content in various media formats.

You can help your child further evaluate photos in this book with additional activities. Look at the images in the book without the What Do You See? feature. Ask your child to describe one detail in each image, such as a color, activity, or setting.

Index

About the Author

Rebecca Felix is a writer and editor from Saint Paul, Minnesota. It is a big city! The city's bridges and tall buildings show many patterns.